Deep Learning, an introduction with two nice short examples

Roland Büchi

Bibliografische Information der Deutschen Nationalbibliothek
Die Deutsche Nationalbibliothek verzeichnet diese Publikation in
der Deutschen Nationalbibliografie; detaillierte bibliografische
Daten sind im Internet über www.dnb.de abrufbar.

Impressum
© Roland Büchi, 2022
Herstellung und Verlag: BoD – Books on Demand,
Norderstedt
ISBN: 978-3-7568-3263-7

Abstract

Artificial intelligence (AI) describes machine processes in which computers provide intelligence similar to that of humans. Machine learning (ML) is a sub-area of AI and describes methods with which such kind of intelligence is provided using data and models. The deep learning, which is described in this booklet, is again a sub-area of ML. It denotes the very frequently used method of how a computer can learn using neural networks and training data and apply what it has learned to other questions similar to the training data.

This booklet introduces the most important basics of deep learning. Two simple about 'one-pager' examples in Python show how training a neural network with forward and back propagation works and how the trained system can process simple forms of artificial thinking. The two short Python programs "Learning truth tables" and "Recognizing a questionnaire" are printed in full and are easy to follow.

1.   Introduction

Neural networks are based on the functioning of the human brain. This consists of around 100 billion nerve cells that can store information. These are connected via synapses, which can pass on this information as signals. When learning, the synapses in the brain are activated and strengthened. This is how information is transmitted from one nerve cell to the other. The number of active synapses and nerve cells are important for learning success. When more nerve cells are involved in the learning process, the information is anchored deeper in the brain. Figure 1 shows a schematic representation of the nerve cells and synapses of the human brain. The number of connections among the 100 billion

($=10^{11}$) neurons is estimated to be 10^{14} or more in total. So every single neuron has connections with 1000 or more other neurons.

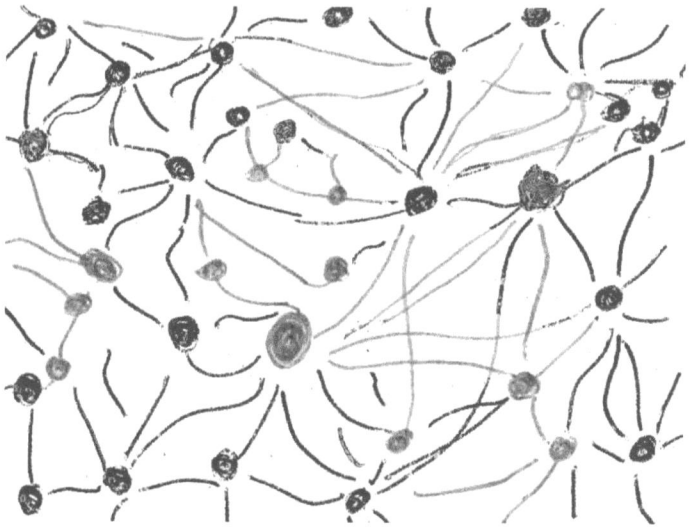

Figure 1: Nerve cells and synapses in the human brain.

Neural networks and deep learning are now technically replicating this situation. In particular, the strengthening of the synapses is of special importance in the training or learning process of such a system. This is a process that is also known from classic control engineering. After a long iterative learning phase, the system converges and the values of the synapses remain constant. A simple neural network is shown in figure 2. If you compare it with the complex structure in the brain, you can easily imagine what incomparably more difficult problems people can successfully deal with. This network will be used later in the booklet to train a simple image recognition problem. First, however, it will be used to show how the replica of the human brain works in a technical sense.

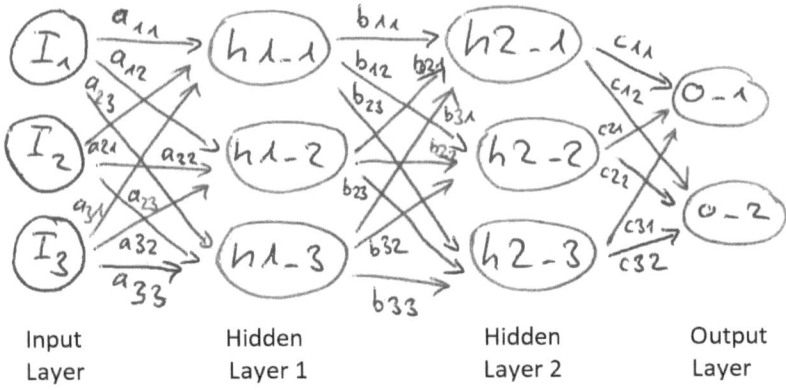

| Input Layer | Hidden Layer 1 | Hidden Layer 2 | Output Layer |

Figure 2: Neural network with two hidden layers.

Every neural network consists of an input and an output layer. It also consists of so-called hidden layers which are not visible from outside. The individual points at these layers are the neurons. The terms neurons or nerve cells are commonly used in the human brain. The connections between the individual neurons are the synapses. Neural networks and deep learning are often associated with image recognition. Projects are known on how this technology can be used to distinguish images of dogs and cats, for example. Later in the booklet such an example is discussed using a simple Python program, although the one there is much simpler. In figure 2, the input layer would then contain features of the image, or in extreme cases, the pixels themselves. The output would then be an output layer for dog and cat recognition, containing a neuron for a recognized cat and a recognized dog.

A comparison of figures 1 and 2 already shows the differences between nature and technology. The connections between the neurons in the human brain are very different and appear to be random. And that is also the subject of current and future research. In contrast, the technical version shows a clear order of the synapses from layer to layer. In general, every neuron in one layer is connected to every neuron in the next layer. In this example, however, there are no connections from a neuron in one layer to the one layer after the next.

The strong limitations of the technical system compared to the natural one can also be seen in the intuitive consideration of the potentials of the neuron and synapse architectures in figure 1 and figure 2. And that's good.

After all, it is intuitively understandable that it should also be possible with the technical neural network to learn at least simple tasks and then to solve them and similar ones.

2. Implementation example: learning truth tables

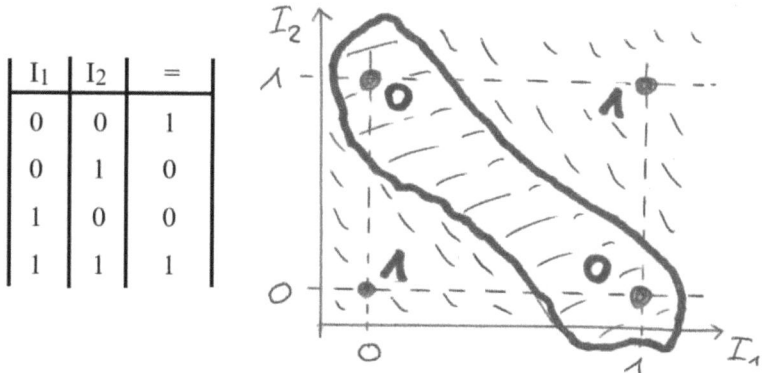

Figure 3: Equivalence function, truth table and graphical representation of the solution with the two inputs on two axes and the values of the outputs.

As a first example, learning truth tables of logic functions with two inputs and one output is discussed and implemented. Figure 3 shows the truth table of the equivalence function and the graphical representation of the solution. The output is exactly then set to 1, if both inputs are the same.

7

At the discussion of the solution it can be shown that the solutions 0 and 1 are not linearly separable. This means that it is not possible to separate the zeros from the ones with just a single straight line. Rather, depending on the drawing, there are either two ones enclosed by a function not equal to a straight line, or two enclosed zeros.

The theory behind this is that at least one hidden layer must be used to learn such a problem. The simplest structure of a neural network that can solve this problem is shown in figure 4.

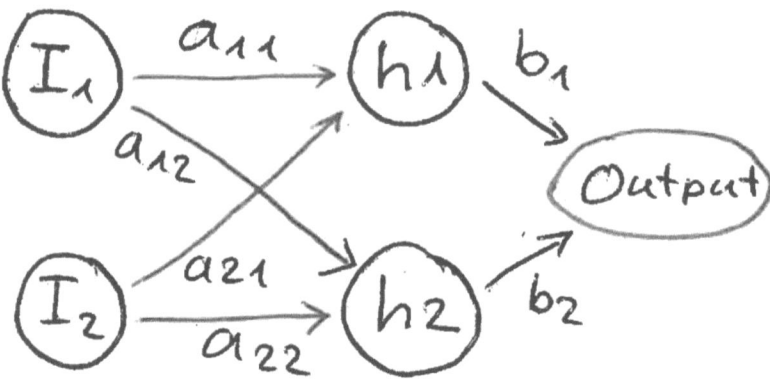

Figure 4: Simplest neural network that can learn a truth table of an equivalence function with two inputs and one output.

Deep learning works as follows in this example: First, the synapses are weighted randomly. According to figure 4, these are the parameters a11, a12, a21, a22, b1 and b2. After that, the first line of the truth table (0,0) is accepted as the pair of values for the two input neurons I1 and I2. From this, the output is computed using forward propagation, discussed below. Then the calculated output is compared to the desired output, here 1. This slightly changes the synapses with the back propagation discussed below. The same is repeated with the second, third and fourth row of the truth table. The whole thing is again repeated several thousand times until the values of the synapses converge.

3. Forward Propagation

Figure 5 shows a single neuron of a layer x_{k1}, i.e. the first neuron of the kth layer and the connections to all neurons of the preceding i^{th} layer. The synapses are z_{11} to z_{n1}.

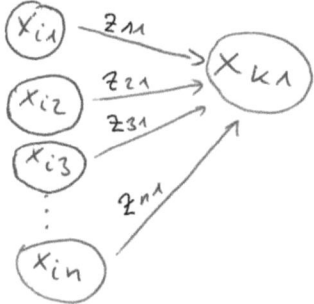

Figure 5: Structure of neurons.

The value of the neurons is analogous to the voltage of the nerve cells in the human brain and is technically calculated using most models as follows:

$$x_{k1} = f\left(\sum_{m=1}^{n} z_{m1} \cdot x_{im}\right) \qquad (1)$$

Since the weights can be positive or negative in the general case, the values of the neurons will also be some negative or positive numbers in the general case. For most models, the value is normalized to a number close to 0 or close to 1. This is achieved using the sigmoid function (2).

$$f(x) = \frac{1}{1 + e^{-\frac{x}{T}}} \qquad (2)$$

A discussion of (2) shows:

$$\lim_{x \to -\infty} f(x) = 0 \qquad \lim_{x \to 0} f(x) = \frac{1}{2} \qquad \lim_{x \to \infty} f(x) = 1 \qquad (3)$$

Figure 6 shows a graphical representation of the sigmoid function. This achieves the desired effect of normalizing the function values to the interval [0...1]. The parameter T only spreads the function and has no influence on the asymptotic function values for x = -∞ or +∞.

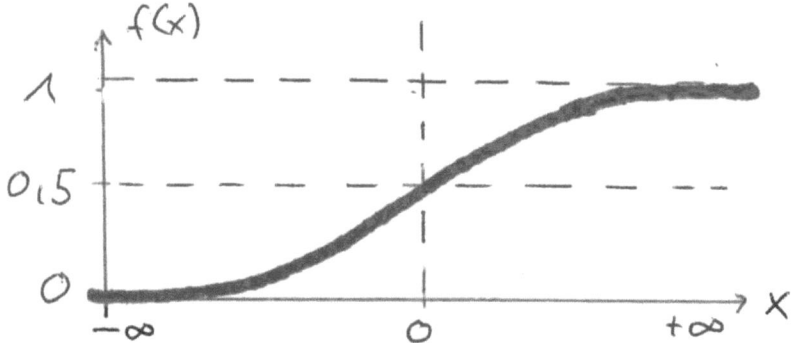

Figure 6: Sigmoid function.

The calculation of the values of the neurons starts with the values of the input layer. Then, using the formulas (1) and (2), all neurons of the next layer, then the next but one layer, etc. are calculated. At the end there are the results of the neurons of the output layer. This calculation is called forward propagation.

4.   Back Propagation

The most important element of a deep learning algorithm is back propagation. This is the core of the actual learning process, which is changing the values of the synapses. For a general synapse z_{qr}, which connects the qth neuron of one layer with the rth neuron of the next layer, the following applies:

$$z_{qr} = z_{qr} + learning\_rate \cdot delta_r \cdot x_q \qquad (4)$$

If it is the last layer, i.e, the output layer, delta_r is calculated to

$$delta_r = x_r \cdot (1 - x_r) \cdot (x_{r\_Training\_data} - x_r) \qquad (5)$$

If it is not the last layer, delta_r is calculated to

$$delta_r = x_r \cdot (1 - x_r) \cdot \sum_{r\_nextlayer} delta_{r\_nextlayer} \cdot z_{r,r\_nextlayer} \qquad (6)$$

Back propagation starts with calculating the rearmost delta_r. Their results are used to calculate those from further in front. Thus, all training data are calculated and then many iterations are carried out. The learning_rate is the weighting of the individual run. If the learning rate is too large, the synapses will not converge asymptotically and oscillations will occur in their values. If it is too small, many iterations have to be carried out in the learning process. This is an effect that is also very well-known from closed loop systems in control engineering. Control engineering also provides stability theories for such systems.

```
#equivalence_deep_learning_example
import random
import math

def sigmoid(x):
    return 1.0 / (1.0 + math.exp(-x))

a11,a12 = random.random(),random.random()
a21,a22 = random.random(),random.random()
b1,b2 = random.random(),random.random()
learning_rate = 0.1
learn_in = [[0,0],[0,1],[1,0],[1,1]]
learn_out = [[1],[0],[0],[1]]

#Learning Algorithm
for _ in range(200000):
    for p in range(4):
        #Forward Propagation
        h1 = sigmoid(a11 * learn_in[p][0] + a21 * learn_in[p][1])
        h2 = sigmoid(a12 * learn_in[p][0] + a22 * learn_in[p][1])
        output = sigmoid(h1 * b1 + h2 * b2)

        #Back Propagation
        delta_o = output*(1-output)*(learn_out[p][0] - output)
        delta_h1 = h1*(1-h1) * delta_o * b1
        delta_h2 = h2*(1-h2) * delta_o * b2
        b1 += learning_rate * delta_o* h1
        b2 += learning_rate * delta_o* h2
        a11 += learning_rate * delta_h1* learn_in[p][0]
        a12 += learning_rate * delta_h2* learn_in[p][0]
        a21 += learning_rate * delta_h1* learn_in[p][1]
        a22 += learning_rate * delta_h2* learn_in[p][1]

#Print Results of learned System
for n in range(4):
    h1 = sigmoid(a11 * learn_in[n][0] + a21 * learn_in[n][1])
    h2 = sigmoid(a12 * learn_in[n][0] + a22 * learn_in[n][1])
    output = sigmoid(h1 * b1 + h2 * b2 )
    print("learning input", learn_in[n], "learning output",
    learn_out[n][0], "calculated", round(output,5))
```

Now you are welcome to play with the example, the code in Python is certainly one of the shortest deep learning programs there is. For example, you can use it to train also other truth tables.

The example with the equivalence was a good starting example to learn the calculations, especially the forward and back propagation. However, there are some limitations. In the case of equivalence, it is intuitively not entirely clear that one can infer further data sets by learning them. Actually, the equivalence is only known from boolean algebra. There are only ones and zeros there. Thus, the present example is already fully determined with a truth table with four rows. In practice, however, deep learning is used precisely to train the neural network with a large set of learning data. Then this is applied to an even larger amount of unknown data. One might ask why one should train the equivalence network with the four known data sets at all in order to then use them to infer the solution of the same four data sets. Of course, one could then use figure 3 to argue that one can use the trained system to infer solutions for the entire spanned area. However, there is a lack of practical relevance here. In addition, the term 'deep learning' in the actual definition is only used when more than one or even many hidden layers are used. Therefore, another example will be discussed in the next chapter. It aims to deepen and expand the knowledge learned in this chapter.

5. Implementation example: recognition of a questionnaire

This chapter discusses the automatic recognition of a handwritten questionnaire using deep learning. In addition, it will also be shown how the entire solution space can be deduced from a limited number of training data. Nevertheless, the example is so simple that both the subset of the training data and the entire solution space are still very easy to understand.

Introduction to the task

The task is to evaluate a handwritten questionnaire with artificial intelligence or, more precisely, with the deep learning approach. Imagine that when you ask a question, you have to differentiate between good and bad. The associated question could be, for example, "How do you like the content of this booklet?"
Now imagine a ready-made questionnaire in which you should put a cross in the right place. This is shown in figure 7. The visual evaluation that we as humans make is of course clear in the two cases above. If the cross is on the left, the answer is "good", if the cross is on the right, the answer is "bad". The case at the bottom is already worth discussing. One could argue that in this case the answer is both "good" and "bad". However, the answer is probably neither of the two, i.e. neither "good" nor "bad". In the following, this is to be learned, calculated and discussed using a deep learning approach.

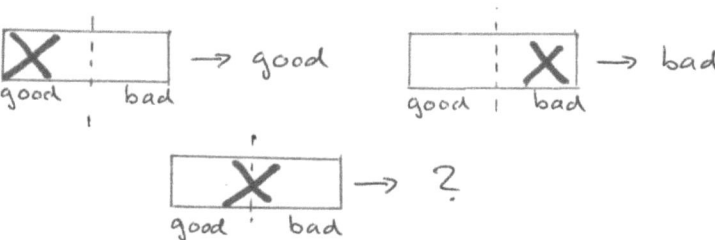

Figure 7: Questionnaire filled out by hand.

As an approach for the implementation, we choose a simplified representation in which the cross is only represented by one bit. In an implementation of the example, one could of course learn many variations of crosses and many positions of them or, in a combination with classic image processing, choose the intersection

14

of the two cross lines as a point. However, since only the core of the implementation with deep learning is discussed here, only three bits according to figure 8 are used as inputs to train the neural network.

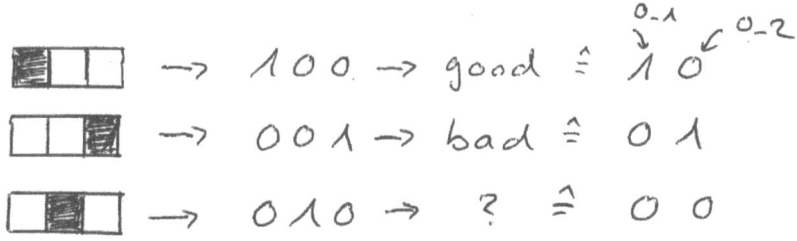

Figure 8: Simplification of the problem to three bits.

Two neurons are used as the output, one for "good" and one for "bad". The neural network is implemented with two hidden layers, each with three neurons as shown in figure 9. It is identical to the one in figure 2. This can still be calculated without special AI libraries.

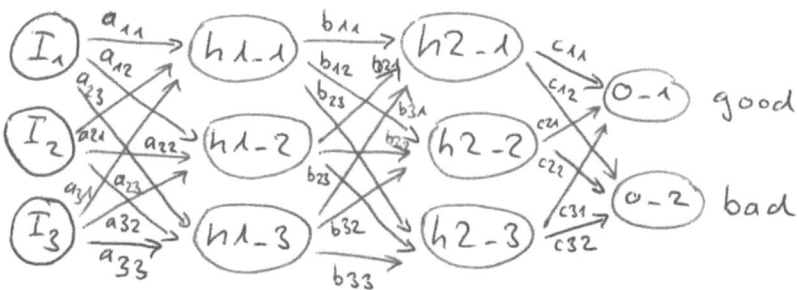

Figure 9: Neural network for questionnaire evaluation with deep learning.

A Python program for solving this problem is as follows.

15

```python
# Deep learning, good bad
# 3 Inputs, 3 Hidden1, 3 Hidden2, 2 Outputs
import random
import math

def sigmoid(x):
    return 1.0 / (1.0 + math.exp(-x))

a11,a12,a13 = random.random(),random.random(),random.random()
a21,a22,a23 = random.random(),random.random(),random.random()
a31,a32,a33 = random.random(),random.random(),random.random()
b11,b12,b13 = random.random(),random.random(),random.random()
b21,b22,b23 = random.random(),random.random(),random.random()
b31,b32,b33 = random.random(),random.random(),random.random()
c11,c12 = random.random(),random.random()
c21,c22 = random.random(),random.random()
c31,c32 = random.random(),random.random()

learn_in = [[1,0,0],[0,0,1],[0,0,0],[1,0,1]]
learn_out = [[1,0],[0,1],[0,0],[0,0]]


learning_rate = 0.1

#Learning Algorithm
for _ in range(20000):
    for p in range(4):
        #Forward Propagation
        h1_1 = sigmoid(a11*learn_in[p][0]+a21*learn_in[p][1]
        +a31*learn_in[p][2])
        h1_2 = sigmoid(a12*learn_in[p][0]+a22*learn_in[p][1]
        +a32*learn_in[p][2])
        h1_3 = sigmoid(a13*learn_in[p][0]+a23*learn_in[p][1]
        +a33*learn_in[p][2])
        h2_1 = sigmoid(b11*h1_1+b21*h1_2+b31*h1_3)
        h2_2 = sigmoid(b12*h1_1+b22*h1_2+b32*h1_3)
        h2_3 = sigmoid(b13*h1_1+b23*h1_2+b33*h1_3)
        o_1 = sigmoid(c11*h2_1+c21*h2_2+c31*h2_3)
        o_2 = sigmoid(c12*h2_1+c22*h2_2+c32*h2_3)

        #Back Propagation
        delta_o1 = o_1*(1-o_1)*(learn_out[p][0] - o_1)
        delta_o2 = o_2*(1-o_2)*(learn_out[p][1] - o_2)
        delta_h2_1 = h2_1*(1-h2_1)*(delta_o1*c11 + delta_o2*c12)
```

```
        delta_h2_2 = h2_2*(1-h2_2)*(delta_o1*c21 + delta_o2*c22)
        delta_h2_3 = h2_3*(1-h2_3)*(delta_o1*c31 + delta_o2*c32)
        delta_h1_1 = h1_1*(1-h1_1) \
        * (delta_h2_1 * b11 + delta_h2_2 * b12 + delta_h2_3 * b13)
        delta_h1_2 = h1_2*(1-h1_2) \
        * (delta_h2_1 * b21 + delta_h2_2 * b22 + delta_h2_3 * b23)
        delta_h1_3 = h1_3*(1-h1_3) \
        * (delta_h2_1 * b31 + delta_h2_2 * b32 + delta_h2_3 * b33)
        c11 += learning_rate * delta_o1 * h2_1
        c12 += learning_rate * delta_o2 * h2_1
        c21 += learning_rate * delta_o1 * h2_2
        c22 += learning_rate * delta_o2 * h2_2
        c31 += learning_rate * delta_o1 * h2_3
        c32 += learning_rate * delta_o2 * h2_3
        b11 += learning_rate * delta_h2_1* h1_1
        b12 += learning_rate * delta_h2_2* h1_1
        b13 += learning_rate * delta_h2_3* h1_1
        b21 += learning_rate * delta_h2_1* h1_2
        b22 += learning_rate * delta_h2_2* h1_2
        b23 += learning_rate * delta_h2_3* h1_2
        b31 += learning_rate * delta_h2_1* h1_3
        b32 += learning_rate * delta_h2_2* h1_3
        b33 += learning_rate * delta_h2_3* h1_3
        a11 += learning_rate * delta_h1_1* learn_in[p][0]
        a12 += learning_rate * delta_h1_2* learn_in[p][0]
        a13 += learning_rate * delta_h1_3* learn_in[p][0]
        a21 += learning_rate * delta_h1_1* learn_in[p][1]
        a22 += learning_rate * delta_h1_2* learn_in[p][1]
        a23 += learning_rate * delta_h1_3* learn_in[p][1]
        a31 += learning_rate * delta_h1_1* learn_in[p][2]
        a32 += learning_rate * delta_h1_2* learn_in[p][2]
        a33 += learning_rate * delta_h1_3* learn_in[p][2]

#Print Results of learned Inputs
for n in range(4):
        h1_1 = sigmoid(a11*learn_in[n][0]
        +a21*learn_in[n][1]+a31*learn_in[n][2])
        h1_2 = sigmoid(a12*learn_in[n][0]
        +a22*learn_in[n][1]+a32*learn_in[n][2])
        h1_3 = sigmoid(a13*learn_in[n][0]
        +a23*learn_in[n][1]+a33*learn_in[n][2])
        h2_1 = sigmoid(b11*h1_1+b21*h1_2+b31*h1_3)
        h2_2 = sigmoid(b12*h1_1+b22*h1_2+b32*h1_3)
        h2_3 = sigmoid(b13*h1_1+b23*h1_2+b33*h1_3)
```

```
        o_1 = sigmoid(c11*h2_1+c21*h2_2+c31*h2_3)
        o_2 = sigmoid(c12*h2_1+c22*h2_2+c32*h2_3)
        print("learned   input",   learn_in[n],   "learned   output",
learn_out[n])
        print("calc o_1: ", round(o_1,5), "calc o_2: ", round(o_2,5))

#Print Results of other Inputs
others_in = [[1,1,0],[0,1,1],[1,1,1],[0,0,0]]
for n in range(4):
        h1_1 = sigmoid(a11*others_in[n][0]
        +a21*others_in[n][1]+a31*others_in[n][2])
        h1_2 = sigmoid(a12*others_in[n][0]
        +a22*others_in[n][1]+a32*others_in[n][2])
        h1_3 = sigmoid(a13*others_in[n][0]
        +a23*others_in[n][1]+a33*others_in[n][2])
        h2_1 = sigmoid(b11*h1_1+b21*h1_2+b31*h1_3)
        h2_2 = sigmoid(b12*h1_1+b22*h1_2+b32*h1_3)
        h2_3 = sigmoid(b13*h1_1+b23*h1_2+b33*h1_3)
        o_1 = sigmoid(c11*h2_1+c21*h2_2+c31*h2_3)
        o_2 = sigmoid(c12*h2_1+c22*h2_2+c32*h2_3)
        print("other input", others_in[n],
        "calc o_1: ", round(o_1,5), "calc o_2: ", round(o_2,5))
```

6.   Discussion

With this problem, one could of course still simply set up a truth table for the 3 bits. This would then have 2^3 = 8 lines, and therefore also 8 combinations. However, the solution space grows very quickly because it would double with each additional pixel. For this reason, from a very small number of pixels, it is no longer possible to work with truth tables and thus cover the entire solution space. However, these eight combinations allow the system to be trained with only a part of the possible combinations. Nevertheless, it remains simple and understandable. In the code you can now choose different training data, for example:

```
learn_in = [[1,0,0],[0,0,1],[0,0,0],[1,0,1]]
```

```
learn_out = [[1,0],[0,1],[0,0],[0,0]]
```

So the system should learn a "good" for the first combination and a "bad" for the second combination. If nothing is filled in, the third combination with only the zeros should deliver neither a "good" nor a "bad" at the output. In the last combination, crosses are set for both "good" and "bad", which should then be evaluated at the output again neither as "good" nor as "bad", i.e. with two zeros.

If you let the system learn this, you train the neural network to deliver good results for these combinations, which are either close to one or close to zero. This is also the case after training the network, as the output shows.

```
learned input [1, 0, 0] learned output [1, 0]
calc o_1:  0.94282 calc o_2:  0.00046
```

```
learned input [0, 0, 1] learned output [0, 1]
calc o_1:  0.00067 calc o_2:  0.94328
```

```
learned input [0, 0, 0] learned output [0, 0]
calc o_1:  0.04276 calc o_2:  0.04191
```

```
learned input [1, 0, 1] learned output [0, 0]
calc o_1:  0.03403 calc o_2:  0.03431
```

Again, no rounding was done after the sigmoid function to show that the calculated outputs are close to zero or one. In contrast to the equivalent function in the other example, the training data here only represent half of all possible combinations. It is now of great interest how this trained neural network copes with the other four unlearned combinations.

other input [1, 1, 0]
calc o_1:   0.94033 calc o_2:   0.00046

other input [0, 1, 1]
calc o_1:   0.00076 calc o_2:   0.92516

other input [1, 1, 1]
calc o_1:   0.05921 calc o_2:   0.01547

other input [0, 1, 0]
calc o_1:   0.09836 calc o_2:   0.01294

The first two inputs, each with the outer and middle pixel, represent a cross in the task, which is drawn slightly over the middle and therefore sets the middle pixel to 1. This is also recognized as "good" or "bad". A closer look at the training data reveals that the middle pixel is always set to 0. Thus, the training data with the set left and right pixels become dominant here. The same can be seen with the solutions for the combination [1,1,1] and [0,1,0]. Here, too, the training data for the two outer pixels were correctly reproduced. Thus it turns out that the middle one, non-learned pixel has no significance for other, non-learned inputs either. If you also want to achieve more significance for the middle pixel, you can also train it explicitly. It is represented by the combination [0,1,0].

learned input [1, 0, 0] learned output [1, 0]
calc o_1:   0.97131 calc o_2:   8e-05

learned input [0, 0, 1] learned output [0, 1]
calc o_1:   0.00033 calc o_2:   0.97069

```
learned input [0, 1, 0] learned output [0, 0]
calc o_1:  0.01805 calc o_2:  0.01575

learned input [1, 0, 1] learned output [0, 0]
calc o_1:  0.02105 calc o_2:  0.01968
```

This results in the same solutions for the combinations that have not been trained as before. You may play with the training data at this point. In many cases, however, the number of training data sets is much smaller than the number of possible input data. If you consider only the first two cases as training data (set range(2) in the code instead of range(4)), the following picture emerges for the untrained data:

```
other input [1, 1, 0]
calc o_1:  0.97257 calc o_2:  0.02728
other input [0, 1, 1]
calc o_1:  0.02983 calc o_2:  0.97039
other input [1, 1, 1]
calc o_1:  0.44736 calc o_2:  0.55186
other input [0, 1, 0]
calc o_1:  0.80429 calc o_2:  0.19514
other input [0, 0, 0]
calc o_1:  0.74893 calc o_2:  0.25107
other input [1, 0, 1]
calc o_1:  0.27444 calc o_2:  0.72573
```

The first two cases are again recognized as "good" or "bad" because the middle pixel was not taken into account in the learning phase. However, since the other combinations with two ones or two zeros in the outer bits were not learned either, the evaluation of this data does not give a clear result for "good" or "bad". If not enough training data can be provided for a problem, the calculated numbers of the neurons themselves are another indicator that can be taken into account in the interpretation.

This example shows very well, that it depends heavily on the quantity and quality of the training data, how well the neural network can be trained for a given problem. In particular, more significant training data with clear solutions are always better than less. This topic is dealt with here only to a very limited extent. However, for a given problem, it is very important to provide a sufficient number of suitable training data.

These two examples impressively show the potential of deep learning in technology. Even with the very small neural networks discussed here, simple examples can be learned with suitable training data, which can also be applied to further unlearned data inputs. The discussion of the last example shows very well that every neural network must be fed with good and significant training data so that it also produces good results for other, non-learned data. However, the neural networks used in today's technical problems are much larger and are also implemented with many hidden layers.

Although this booklet could only give a first introduction, the author hopes that some fundamental properties could be shown and that everyone who worked through the examples could get a good introduction to the topic.

7.   Literature

[1] Rosenblatt, Frank. "The perceptron: a probabilistic model for information storage and organization in the brain." *Psychological review* 65.6 (1958): 386

[2] Ivakhnenko, Alekseĭ Grigor'evich, and Valentin Grigorévich Lapa. *Cybernetic predicting devices*. PURDUE UNIV LAFAYETTE IND SCHOOL OF ELECTRICAL ENGINEERING, 1966.

[3] Steinbuch, Karl. "Die lernmatrix." *Kybernetik* 1.1 (1961): 36-45

[4] Fukushima, Kunihiko, and Sei Miyake. "Neocognitron: A self-organizing neural network model for a mechanism of visual pattern recognition." *Competition and cooperation in neural nets*. Springer, Berlin, Heidelberg, 1982. 267-285.

[5] Dechter, Rina. "Learning while searching in constraint-satisfaction problems." (1986): 178-185.

[6] LeCun, Yann, et al. "Backpropagation applied to handwritten zip code recognition." *Neural computation* 1.4 (1989): 541-551.

[7] Büchi, Roland. *Modellierung und Regelung von Impact Drives für Positionierungen im Nanometerbereich*. Diss. ETH Zurich, 1996

[8] Waibel, Alexander, et al. "Phoneme recognition using time-delay neural networks." *IEEE transactions on acoustics, speech, and signal processing* 37.3 (1989): 328-339.

[9] Russel, Stuart J, Norvig, Peter, Artificial Intelligence: A Modern Approach (2nd edition), Upper Saddle River, New Jersey: Prentice Hall, pp 111- 114, ISBN 0-13-790395-2, 2003.

[10] Ritter, Helge, Thomas Martinetz, and Klaus Schulten. *Neural computation and self-organizing maps: an introduction.* Reading, MA: Addison-Wesley, 1992.

[11] Büchi, Roland. *State space control, LQR and observer: step by step introduction with Matlab examples.* Norderstedt Books on Demand, 2010.

[12] Kubat, Miroslav. "Neural networks: a comprehensive foundation by Simon Haykin, Macmillan, 1994, ISBN 0-02-352781-7." *The Knowledge Engineering Review* 13.4 (1999): 409-412.

[13] Behnke, Sven. *Hierarchical neural networks for image interpretation.* Vol. 2766. Springer, 2003.

[14] Schulz, H., and S. Behnke. "Deep learning-layer-wise learning of feature hierarchies. Künstliche Intelligenz. 26 (4), 357–363 (2012)."

[15] Buechi, Roland, et al. "Fully autonomous mobile mini-robot." *Microrobotics and Micromechanical Systems.* Vol. 2593. SPIE, 1995.

[16] Hertz, John, Anders Krogh, and Richard G. Palmer. *Introduction to the theory of neural computation.* CRC Press, 2018.